PROVIDENCE & DESTINY

The Nicholas Duncan-Williams Story

ARCHBISHOP N. DUNCAN-WILLIAMS

PROVIDENCE AND DESTINY
The Archbishop Nicholas Duncan-Williams Story

ISSN: 2026 6952

Copyright ©2015 Nicholas Duncan-Williams

No part of this book may be reproduced, shared in a retrieval system or transmitted in any form or by any means, electronic, mechanical, photocopying, recording without prior written permission of the Author/Publisher

For further enquiries and for training materials,
please contact the address below:
Action Chapel International
P. O. Box K.A. 9527
Airport, Accra, Ghana
Tel: 024 2643588
Email: archbishop1@actionchapel.net

Published by:
Action Chapel International
P. O. Box K.A. 9527
Airport, Accra, Ghana
Tel: 024 2643588

Printed in Ghana by:
TYPE CO. LTD.
+233. 30 223.2252

DOMINION TELEVISION
is now on air 24/7!

Winning Souls - Changing Lives

INFO:

Catch us live on Multi TV Channel 5
For more information on DTV

Call 0302.745.000 or visit
info@newdtv.com

www.actionchapel.net

ACTION CHAPEL PRAYER CATHEDRAL
SERVICE TIMES
SPINTEX ROAD, ACCRA

SUNDAY MORNING SERVICES
7 am - 9:30 am
10 am - 12:30 pm

EVERY 1st SUNDAY EVENING SERVICE
6 pm - 8:30 pm

WEDNESDAY (MIDWEEK) SERVICE:
6:30 pm - 8:30 pm

DOMINION HOUR (Thursdays):
9 am - 12 noon

MORNING GLORY (Saturdays):
7 am – 9:30 am

FIRM FOUNDATION SUNDAY SERVICES:
7 am – 9:30 am
10 am – 12:30 pm

For Action branches, fellowship, and other church activities, Please call +233.302.745.000, Or visit www.actionchapel.net

FOLLOW ME ON FACEBOOK!

https://www.facebook.com/archbishopduncanwilliams

TABLE OF CONTENTS

Chapters

Chapter 1: Introduction   1

Chapter 2: Born For Purpose   8
My Birth   8

Chapter 3: The School Years   14
Bolgatanga Market   15
Back To Accra   17

Chapter 4: My Father's House   24
Sense of Destiny   25
The Importance of a Father   27

Chapter 5: Stowaway Lessons   30
Stowaway to France   30
Sent Back Home   34
Stowaway To Israel   35

Chapter 6: Altars of Sacrifice   37
The Executioner   37
Divine Escapes   39
Looking For God   43

Chapter 7: Pain Reveals a New Beginning   46
The Traditions of Men   46
My Hand in the Fire   48

Chapter 8: Salvation   51
The Bed of Affliction   51
Salvation Comes   52

Chapter 9: A New Life in Christ	54
Bible School in Benin City	54
Church of Pentecost	56
Ministry Beginnings	57
Chapter 10: The Birth of Christian Action Faith Ministries	60
The Various Locations	60
Historic Recognition	61
Chapter 11: What To Do In Times of Crisis	63
Crisis Can Happen in Ministry	63
Offenses and Mastering Betrayal	64
Final Advice When Crisis Comes	65
Chapter 12: Pray With Me	67
Prayer Points	67
Prayer of Salvation	68

Dedication

I dedicate this book to my wife Rosa, my four children, my two sons-in-law, and my five grandchildren.

I am especially grateful to all of my spiritual children worldwide who have stood with me through the test of time. It is because of them that I am a father. I want to take this opportunity to thank them. Their loyalty and dedication have not gone unnoticed and I am grateful for all of them that have remained and continue to stand with me.

"And the servant abideth not in the house forever: but the Son abideth ever." (John 8:35)

CHAPTER 01

INTRODUCTION

"For I know the thoughts that I think toward you, saith the Lord, thoughts of peace, and not of evil, to give you an expected end." (Jeremiah 29:11)

Over the years many people have asked me the key to my success. They have also asked me if I believe that I am chosen by God. Throughout my life, I have had to ask myself what makes a man successful. I have come to believe that success is not determined by how you start or where you are now. Success is defined by how you end. I have discovered that God's definition of success and man's definition are not the same. I will not know if I have been successful until I finish the race and hear the Lord's assessment of my life.

Men can indeed be chosen by God. But, it is a man's decision to choose to follow God and be faithful until the end that will determine whether he finds good success. God's definition of success is not attached to human reasoning, human skill or human assessments. God's definition of success is attached to the assignment he has given you – whether it is to lead or to follow. Take for example what the scripture says about Moses's divine helpers, Joshua, Aaron and Hur:

> *"So Joshua did as Moses had said to him, and fought with Amalek: and Moses, Aaron, and Hur went up to the top of the hill. And it came to pass, when Moses held up his hand, that Israel prevailed: and when he let down his hand, Amalek prevailed. But Moses 'hands were heavy; and they took a stone, and put it under him, and he sat thereon; and Aaron and Hur stayed up his hands, the one on the one side, and the other on the other side; and his hands were steady until the going down of the sun." (Exodus 17:10-12)*

The success of Joshua on the battlefield was not the same requirement for Aaron and Hur to lift up the hands of Moses. They did not participate in the battle, but it was their obedience to keep their assignment and all of them working together in their various roles that gave Israel the victory over the Amalekites. If they had not kept their assignment an entire generation would have been lost.

We must keep our assignment if we will have success in God.

> *"This book of the law shall not depart out of thy mouth; but thou shalt meditate therein day and night, that thou mayest observe to do*

according to all that is written therein:for then thou shalt make thy way prosperous, and then thou shalt have good success." (Joshua 1:8)

It is obedience to what God instructs us to do that makes us successful in God.

As I recount the story of my life in this book, I pray you will understand that you are indeed chosen by God, but that in order to be successful, you must also choose to serve God until the end. It is remembering where I have come from and the circumstances of my life that have helped me remain humble after forty years of preaching to nations across the world. As I look back over my journey, I realize with great amazement that the Hand of God was at work in my life from the very beginning.

Scripture tells us that God makes selections that are not based on human requirements. God does not consult your past to determine your future. In fact, God makes selections and determinations before you even have a past. I believe it is for these reasons that God repeatedly reminded King David of his lowly beginnings. Before he became ruler of Israel, he was a mere shepherd boy. The word written declares:

"I will praise thee; for I am fearfully and wonderfully made: marvellous are thy works; and that my soul knoweth right well. My substance was not hid from thee, when I was

> *made in secret, and curiously wrought in the lowest parts of the earth. Thine eyes did see my substance, yet being unperfect; and in thy book all my members were written, which in continuance were fashioned, when as yet there was none of them."* **(Psalm 139:14-16)**

God thinks about you and me and He has His own plan for our lives. Jeremiah 29:11 says, ***"For I know the thoughts that I think toward you, saith the Lord, thoughts of peace, and not of evil, to give you an expected end."***

God decides without consultation with anyone what a man should be in his life. Jeremiah 1:5 says, ***"Before I formed thee in the belly I knew thee; and before thou camest forth out of the womb I sanctified thee, and I ordained thee a prophet unto the nations."***

It is God who decides our destiny, but He gives us the option to make our own choices. It is those choices that either lead us away from or closer towards our destiny. God shows us life and death; good and evil and He will even tell us which way to go, but ultimately the choice is ours to make. Deuteronomy 30:19 says:

> *" I call heaven and earth to record this day against you, that I have set before you life and death, blessing and cursing: therefore choose life, that both thou and thy seed may live...."*

These Scriptures show us that God makes us and He has a plan for us. But, beloved, the devil also has a plan for us and he will assign situations, circumstances and agents of destruction to enforce his plan. But, rest assured, God will also give us divine assistance through the circumstances of our life, through angelic intervention and human compassion to lead us to the plan that He has for us.

> *"And hath made of one blood all nations of men for to dwell on all the face of the earth, and hath determined the times before appointed, and the bounds of their habitation..." (Acts 17:26)*

My life is a testimony. Your life is a testimony. God has a plan for me and His purpose for me was already predetermined. All He was looking for was my willing cooperation with His plan. The enemy has a plan to destroy you and all he is looking for is your willing cooperation with that plan. You will see in my story that as long as I was unaware of God's plan, the enemy was determined to derail the divine plan that God has for my life. But, once I made the choice to follow the plan of God, to cooperate with the Lord and to seek Him with all my heart, soul and strength, my life dramatically changed and my divine destiny unfolded before me. He opened the door of deliverance for me and countless others. God took me out of the miry clay, set my feet fast upon the rock, and put a song in my mouth to sing:

> *"He brought me up also out of an horrible pit, out of the miry clay, and set my feet upon a rock, and established my goings. And he hath put a new song in my mouth, even praise*

unto our God: many shall see it, and fear, and shall trust in the Lord." (Psalm 40:2-3)

Beloved, I owe it all to the Lord Jesus Christ. He is the one who has made all the difference in my life!

You must make a choice whom you will serve. Today you are the sum total of all the choices you have ever made in your life. Whether good or evil, the choices you have made do not make you a failure or a success. A failure is only a true failure if you do not learn from the mistake. But, every failure has the potential to become a success, if you learn and make a different choice the next time. Nelson Mandela said, "Do not judge me by my successes, judge me by how many times I fell down and got back up again."

The next choice you make can determine your future. I encourage you as you read this book, to choose to serve the Lord on a deeper level. Choose to pray more, to love more, to serve the Lord in every way.

Do not let your circumstances, where you come from or what people believe about you, stop you from fulfilling God's purpose for your life. You, too, can have a story to tell if you believe God's Word.

It is my prayer that as you read this book, the Holy Ghost will cause the blindness and deception over your spiritual eyes to be lifted, and that there shall come a supernatural quickening of your spirit man to stand tall and become a battle axe in the hand of the Almighty God in the realm of the spirit. It is also my prayer that not only will your prayer life change dramatically, but that you will pray so fervently that there will be miraculous and supernatural changes in your personal life, that of your family, and your local church.

I urge you to read this book prayerfully and with expectancy as God reveals truths to you that will break strongholds in your life. Remember you are receiving information that the enemy does not want you to have. An enemy exposed is a dangerous foe. No doubt he will attempt to throw you off your path by intimidation or an outright attack. I urge you to keep yourself covered with prayer as you press forward, holding fast to God's promise that we are more than conquerors through Christ Jesus.

In this end time, it is those with the capacity to break the power of hell that will move forward and achieve the deep purposes of God concerning their lives. You now have a God-given opportunity; take it and run.

The Psalmist Andre Crouch sang:

> *"Through it all I have learned to trust in Jesus*
> *I have learned to trust in God*
> *I have learned to depend upon His Word."*

CHAPTER 02

BORN FOR PURPOSE

"He hath made every thing beautiful in his time: also he hath set the world in their heart, so that no man can find out the work that God maketh from the beginning to the end." (Ecc. 3:11)

My Birth

The story of the circumstances under which I was born is a clear indication that to accomplish His purpose, God overrules the schemes and designs of the enemy. Beloved, I want you to know, through the telling of my own story, that the circumstances of your birth are not a prediction of your future.

I was not aware of the circumstances of my birth until a conversation with my mother as an adult. She pulled me to the side one day and said to me, "Nicholas, have I ever told you what travails I endured to give birth to you?"

Curiously, I replied, "Mama, what is it that you have not told me all these years about my birth?"

"Sit down please," she said to me, directing me to a large chair.

"I daily bless the Name of the Lord for your life and His call upon you," she said.

"Whenever I look back more than three decades ago and recollect it all, I see the finger of God in your life both to preserve and to use you."

My mother went on to recount how she battled through months of bleeding after she conceived me. At one point she became so ill, the doctors advised her to undergo a D&C procedure for her own life, as they believed the pregnancy was not viable. After the procedure she continued to bleed, but to the glory of God she went into labor at nine months and successfully gave birth to a healthy baby boy she named Nicholas.

God has a way of covering great destinies in challenging births. Moses, David, Esther, and countless others marked for greatness were born through great adversity. God sent reinforcements, angelic assistance and human compassion to intervene in the lives of those great men and women and He did the same for me.

There are people who are born rich, but still struggle to find their purpose. There are people who are born in great difficulty and it is the adversities of life that help them search earnestly for the reason for which they were born. Zechariah 4:10 says,*"Do not despise small beginnings, for the Lord rejoices to see the work begin..." (NLT).*

Beloved, the circumstances of your birth and early childhood may make you feel rejected, despised or overlooked or you may consider yourself as a misfit or an outcast. But, I want to encourage you today that regardless of the circumstances of your birth, you can prevail and overcome the vicissitudes of life through a life in Christ Jesus. The enemy will always attempt to use the circumstances of our birth to determine the outcome of our future. But the Word of God says,

> *"But we speak the wisdom of God in a mystery, even the hidden wisdom, which God ordained before the world unto our glory: Which none of the princes of this world knew: for had they known it, they would not have crucified the Lord of glory." (1 Cor. 2:7-8)*

The devil can sense and tell timing and seasons when greatness is revealed and he will execute a plan to destroy the seed of greatness when the signs appear. When it was time for the promise God gave to deliver the Jews from Egyptian bondage, the devil deployed Pharaoh in Exodus 1, but God used His Hand of providence to deliver Moses and save him alive in Exodus 2.

In Genesis chapter 3, God promised that the Deliverer would be male and born of a woman (Genesis 3:15) and when it was time the Star of Jesus was seen by wise men who alerted Herod and the enemy used Herod in Matthew 2 to enact a law to kill all the male seed. Generation to generation the enemy hasn't changed. The difficult circumstances under which you were born, just may be an indication of the prophetic promise over your life. Do not lose hope! If he cannot stop you from being born, he will do everything he can to prevent you from discovering the will of God for your life and eventually kill you.

> *"The thief comes only to steal and kill and destroy; I have come that they may have life, and have it to the full."(John 10:10)*

He is an accuser and he will quote the negative circumstances of your life to frustrate you and to make you walk in fear so that your life will not work out. But, it is the confession of your faith in God that will destroy the voice of fear in your life.

> *"Then he showed me Joshua the high priest standing before the angel of the LORD, and Satan standing at his right hand to accuse him. The LORD said to Satan, "The LORD rebuke you, Satan! Indeed, the LORD who has chosen Jerusalem rebuke you! Is this not a brand plucked from the fire?" (Zechariah 3:1-2)*

There is the human tendency to hold things against others for the wrongs they once did to us. Naturally there are even things we can hold against God or our parents or other adults as it relates to the circumstances of our birth and childhood. Some people may not have offended us directly but we still have some things against them. Perhaps for their rejection and silence whilst we trod the painful paths of life's difficulties. But bitterness can put us in an adversarial relationship with God and ourselves. Bitterness corrodes the container that holds it. A wise man once said unforgiveness is like drinking poison and expecting the other person to die.

Nelson Mandela made a profound statement after he had spent twenty seven years sleeping on the bare cold floors of the prison rooms of South Africa: "As I walked out the door toward the gate that would lead to my freedom, I knew if I didn't leave my bitterness and hatred behind, I'd still be in prison."

One would have thought that he would repay the men behind the brutal system who had put him in jail when he became the first black president of South Africa. But he never did. Why? The bigger picture. Your life is bigger than your present circumstances. Release others and forgive them so that you can be truly free. This is difficult to do and may not make sense to the human mind - but the ways of God are not the ways of man. Matthew 6:15 as well as Mark 11:25 tells us,

> *"But if ye forgive not men their trespasses, neither will your Father forgive your trespasses."*
>
> *"And when ye stand praying, forgive, if ye have ought against any: that your Father also which is in heaven may forgive you your trespasses."*

I emphasized any. Any means any. No explanation justifies unforgiveness.

Can you look at the bigger picture in relation to your relationships, family, friends, church and your nation? What can you forgive to strengthen the relationship? Or will you hold back and let your Godly relationships and divine connections be destroyed?

Forgiveness does not mean you should trust the person again, but you must forgive them and release them because forgiveness is for you – so that your prayers will be heard. You do not have to necessarily rejoin them, but you must let them receive your forgiveness.

> *Do not grieve the Holy Spirit of God, by whom you were sealed for the day of redemption. Let all bitterness and wrath and anger and clamor and slander be put away from you, along with all malice. Be kind to one another, tender-hearted, forgiving each other, just as God in Christ also has forgiven you. (Ephesians 4:30-32)*

CHAPTER 03

THE SCHOOL YEARS

"And not only so, but we glory in tribulations also: knowing that tribulation worketh patience; And patience, experience; and experience, hope..." (Romans 5:3-4)

Because I grew up with my mother in a single parent household and with six brothers and sisters it made my early childhood development very difficult. I realize now, it was a demonic programming to frustrate the will of God for my life and throw me off course to my destiny. These early circumstances stifled my education. I eventually enrolled in school at a rather advanced age compared to my classmates — I was a clear four years older than the next oldest student in my class. The constant taunting and teasing was uncomfortable and did not give me a sense of belonging.

The circumstances of my late entry into school and the fact that I was constantly fighting with other children embarrassed my mother and I decided I would not attend school any longer. As a result my mother chose to make a difficult decision. We moved to Wa in the Upper Region of Ghana. The harsh realities of life and deprivation began to take their toll on me. My only consolation in Wa was that a large number of my classmates were also far older than the stipulated age. This gave me some breathing space for a brief moment. But, after awhile the same thing started happening. I was fighting all the time.

As a result of the demands of my mother's profession as a nurse, coupled with the fact that I was constantly fighting and being put out of schools, we transferred to Bolgatanga from Wa. But unfortunately, this move did not change my situation significantly. If anything, it presented me with new levels of hardships to endure. In fact, I spent my initial year there at home.

Bolgatanga Market

Faced with financial difficulties, I decided that it was time to go to work to support myself. This was not easy. I struck a bargain with local newspaper vendors who each day supplied me with bulk copies of the daily newspapers. Further supplies from vendors obviously depended on my integrity in making prompt returns, as well as my talent as a salesman. Each morning, well before daybreak, I took a quick bath and, whistling discordantly to keep my spirits up, I set off for work. By sheer drive and determination, I soon established myself as the "Accra boy" who made incredible sales.

Soon after I started working, I used the money I had earned from my sales to help my mother and my siblings. Every morning, as soon as my newspaper sales were over, I trotted home and wore my school uniform and went to school. Slowly and with great determination I overcame my inability to support myself while in school. There is no denying that the presence of large sums of money in the hands of a schoolboy can have a negative influence on him. In fact, my newspaper sales adversely affected my schoolwork. This was exacerbated by the enticement to work longer hours so that I could afford to buy personal items.

To increase my income, I took on one more responsibility - pushing wooden food carriage trucks. This generated more income for me in spite of the strain on my young body. The truck pushing business in the Bolgatanga market was a highly competitive one. It called for all the imagination and creativity I could muster. For days, I worked assiduously on my hired food carriage truck. I painted it with bright colors. With all my youthful artistry, I made awkward designs on the front and sides to attract customers. My efforts yielded the desired results. Buyers wrestled over who would benefit from my beautifully decorated carrier. In a matter of weeks, I had established my position as a hardworking food carriage truck pusher all over the Bolgatanga market.

One day I received some discouraging news about my newspaper sales business. The proprietors had gone bankrupt and had decided to wind up the business. Then, the owner of my food truck called me over a few mornings after the newspaper sales ended. "Small Nick," he said, with his hand gently tapping my quivering shoulders. "Eh, due to some problems I'm encountering, I have decided to withdraw the truck and move out of town."

I was momentarily dazed by the full implication of his words. I bowed my head and I cried tears of despair. Anguish engulfed me. After a short while, he said to me, "Goodbye, Nick, and God help you." With that, he left, taking his truck with him.

I cannot recall how long I stood there watching him push the truck away. I headed home downcast and withdrew into bed and lay down for hours analyzing the events of my life. Fortunately, my mother somehow managed to raise enough money to cover my needs, thereby easing my agony over the closure of my businesses.

Back To Accra

Eventually we left Bolgatanga and my family returned to Accra where my mother had been transferred. I felt a welcome relief because I knew that the capital city would offer much better business opportunities.

Life and business in Accra were certainly different from Bolgatanga. A whole range of ideas rolled through my mind and school no longer held my interest. The reason was simple - I had outgrown it. I was no longer in a mood to tolerate the taunting and jeers of my fellow students who felt that I was far too big for my class.

I was determined to make up quickly in Accra all that I had lost in Bolgatanga. Several times, I strolled through the teaming crowd of pedestrians, visitors, sellers and buyers. I carefully surveyed the land for a couple of weeks. Then, I made my move. Eventually I embarked on the business of selling "P.K." a popular chewing gum to the afternoon cinemagoers at the Opera Square. I sold the P.K. for a watchman (a security guard) at the movie theatre for a percentage and I could watch all the movies for free. This was brisk business, but obviously not enough to sustain me. Therefore, I started to go over to the Accra Central train station early in the morning where I helped to carry bags of foodstuffs for a fixed fee. Late in the evenings, to save money, I walked the nearly ten-kilometer distance to Kokomlemle, a suburb in Accra where I was living with my uncle who had offered to put me up in his garage. At cock's crow, I would crawl out of the garage and hurry to the Accra Central train station. The new friends I made there introduced me to gambling. This was a welcome escape from the nightly loneliness of my garage apartment and provided better company than my nighttime companions: the cockroaches which raced fiercely in the darkness around my bed.

My mother decided to send me to a trade school and I refused to attend even though she was willing to pay my school fees. She was so exasperated; she decided to turn me in to the juvenile court system. I was remanded to the court of Justice Ananse who was going to send me to serve a term in the juvenile penal system. However, when he saw my last name was Duncan-Williams, he inquired if I was the son of the politician Duncan-Williams. I had not seen my father in all this time.

My father was summoned to the court and I was released to go and live with my father. My father, a former politician who eventually became an ambassador, lived at the Airport Residential Area. This marked the beginning of events that were to alter the course of my life.

Beloved, there are times and seasons in life that when you are going through them, God is using the hardships to develop your character and strength of perseverance. The Scripture tells us that tribulation worketh patience, and patience experience, and experience hope (Romans 5:3-4). It is the tribulations I suffered as a young man that helped develop certain character traits that have shown me by experience that trouble does not last always and that situations change. In all the childhood struggles, I developed hope. I had a picture in my mind of a better future and even though circumstances beyond my control caused me to struggle in school, life was providing experiences that trained me and helped me develop the discipline to work hard. I was willing to go to work to obtain the things I hoped for. My work ethic was borne from this season of adversity. I now realize that although many onlookers from the outside may have thought I was a failure, God was using the seemingly failures to develop a sense of character and resilience that would help me in future days to come.

The battle over your life is not over your intellectual gifts or the material acquisitions, but rather over the divine purpose you are destined to fulfill on this earth. I was in a battle before I even knew I had anything worth fighting for!

Let me establish one important fact: Satan and his forces do not know the exact purposes of God concerning you in a particular area until the purposes are revealed by prophecy. The very moment God's agenda for our lives is revealed and his intentions are made known, the enemy takes measures in the realm of the spirit and the natural to hinder the manifestations of the prophecies. So if we fold our arms and say: "God said it, it shall surely come to pass," without praying it into manifestation, the prophecy could be challenged by the forces of darkness.

In order for the plan of God to be carried out in the Earth, God needs a body. *"Wherefore when he cometh into the world, he saith, Sacrifice and offering thou wouldest not, but a body hast thou prepared me..." (Hebrews 10:5).* In the same way, the enemy makes plans and he can deploy human vessels to execute those plans. The enemy used Pharaoh against Moses and Herod against Jesus. God in His Divine providence deployed Miriam, the sister of Moses, to help hide baby Moses and Joseph, the husband of Mary, to help protect the baby Jesus.

There were so many forces working against me – even from birth, from without and within...but for God! It is only the providence of God and His purpose for my life that kept me from being destroyed.

Children carrying prophetic destiny can become targets of spiritual assassins and without spiritual parents and divine intervention their lives can be destroyed. This is why as parents we must be connected to the throne room of the Father through prayer and intercession. We must also teach our children to pray and fight for their God-given destiny. We must never give up and find ourselves sleeping on prophetic words that have been spoken over their lives.

We must guard against the common mistake many believers make of rejoicing, dancing, and then *sleeping* when we receive prophecies from the Lord.

We must counter the lie that somehow the prophecy will come to pass automatically. It is not so!

Every prophecy is conditional. For example of the prophecy in Judges 13 about the life of one of Israel's great judges - Samson – was a prophecy that was conditional. He was to be a Nazarite (Judges 13:3-5) and when he violated the Nazarite Law by getting his hair cut in Judges 16:16-20 his destiny was aborted and he died prematurely (Judges 16:30).

It is the most dangerous path to tread to ignore, misunderstand or take lightly the prophetic word because the revealed purpose will prompt an attack from Satan. As far as Satan is concerned, God has openly declared His intentions concerning His child in a particular area, and the enemy is not going to sit down and watch that prophecy materialize. So he begins to set roadblocks and raise barriers to frustrate the person so that the true purpose never comes to pass. If we fail to understand this, we may become angry and frustrated with God and doubt His word and plan for our lives. Many walk away from the faith defeated not knowing that they must contend and pray earnestly for the manifestation of the promise of God concerning their life.

> *"This charge I commit unto thee, son Timothy, according to the prophecies which went before on thee, that thou by them mightest war a good warfare..." (1st Timothy 1:18)*

What has God said concerning your life? Beloved, you must contend through prayer for the full manifestation. Contend means to fight for what God has already willed for your life. Satan is contesting your Father's Will and you must stand and fight otherwise you will cede your inheritance to the enemy and you stand to lose the promise. You must contend for the Father's Will for your life.

> *"But when the fulness of the time was come, God sent forth his Son, made of a woman, made under the law, To redeem them that were under the law, that we might receive the adoption of sons. And because ye are sons, God hath sent forth the Spirit of his Son into your hearts, crying, Abba, Father. Wherefore thou art no more a servant, but a son; and if a son, then an heir of God through Christ." (Gal. 4:4-7)*

CHAPTER 04

MY FATHER'S HOUSE

"Look to Abraham your father And to Sarah who gave birth to you in pain; When he was but one I called him, Then I blessed him and multiplied him." (Isaiah 51:2)

My father was in a "no-nonsense" mood concerning my explanations about my inability to return to the classroom. He was at a loss of what to do with me - I was meeting him after all this time and we did not really know one another. It was not an easy transition for either one of us. He decided to deposit me in an elementary school in Madina, a neighborhood in Accra. It did not take me too long to discover that I was not inspired by the teachers or the classroom setting. Too many societal influences had firmly gripped me: the fast life, the discos and the blazing voices of the "Highlife" musicians. I could not concentrate on my studies when my heart was elsewhere. One day I walked out never to go back again. I was determined to seek validation outside of school.

This time the sound of the airplanes attracted me. I soon made a large company of friends by helping air travelers check their luggage and by assisting them with whatever other miscellaneous assignments I could find. I established myself at the airport as a self-appointed travel agent.

Sense of Destiny

As the days turned from weeks into months, I began to realize through my interactions with travellers, airport staff and others that there had to be more to life. I became acutely aware of a new sense of awakening coming over me. It was like stirring up out of a stupor to discover you are the child of a king, a prince, without even knowing it. How can I express to you the feeling that I experienced? It was like a veil was pulled off my mind as, through my gloom of hopelessness, I began to dimly comprehend that life could offer so much more. A new sense of destiny seized me, and I could neither wriggle out of it nor comprehend its meaning. Worst of all, my position as a *'goroboy'* or airport attendant, did not align with this new uncomfortable realization.

I began to re-examine my life. I felt within my heart that new experiences and new horizons lay in store for me. But what? I did not know! In the same vein, I realized that there were also some strong forces determined to destroy my life. I began to truly awaken that life – my life – must have a deeper meaning. I was determined to explore and see what else life had to offer. It is with these thoughts in my heart that I went to see my father about my new intentions.

One evening, I walked into my father's presence as he reclined on the sofa gazing at the sunset. He took one cursory glance at me and returned his gaze to the sunset. It was clear to me from our limited interaction that he considered me a wayward young man - listless, hopeless, a failure waiting to happen. That was certainly not God's opinion of me -- but I did not know and could not discern it then. Before I could state my purpose, he asked, "What do you want?" I pulled myself together quickly as my thoughts ran haywire.

I stammered a reply: "Please, I want to talk to you about my plans to go to America." With a loud cough of derision, he retorted, "Alright, thanks for coming. I'll see you later." All the while, he had not as much as stolen a second glance at me. With heaviness of heart, I slammed the door behind me.

I left my father's presence and room with the resolute determination to prove him wrong. In that moment, I made a vow to myself: "I must pay any price to succeed in life," I swore, making no secret of it to my street friends. This would prove to be a pivotal moment in my life.

The Importance of a Father

Beloved, each one of us, whether male or female, gets their identity from their father. When we are born, we usually carry our father's last name. In many cultures, it is fathers who name the children. It is the patriarchal DNA that determines the sex of an embryo. Fatherhood gives the individual a sense of identity. Everyone traces his or her roots back to his parents, especially to the father. This should not be strange because God gave the father the responsibility of sowing the seed of each individual who comes into the world. Father means source, the beginning and the originator.

> *"Look to Abraham your father And to Sarah who gave birth to you in pain; When he was but one I called him, Then I blessed him and multiplied him." (Isaiah 51:2)*

I have heard many stories from people who have lived with a sense of emptiness their whole life because they did not know who their father was or who do not have a good relationship with their father. Fatherhood is very critical to the stability of humanity and therefore cannot be overlooked or taken for granted.

The Bible says in Ephesians 6:4, ***"And, ye fathers, provoke not your children to wrath: but bring them up in the nurture and admonition of the Lord."*** In fact that passage (Ephesians 6:1-4) speaks to children to obey and to honor their parents and then Apostle Paul specifically addresses the father, but not the mother. This is because the role of the father is critical in defining the success of the family. Children must listen to and obey their parents because God has given your parents keys that will unlock your purpose and give you success for your future. God testified about Abraham's ability as a father to raise up his children:

> *"For I know him, that he will command his children and his household after him, and they shall keep the way of the LORD, to do justice and judgment; that the LORD may bring upon Abraham that which he hath spoken of him." (Genesis 18:19)*

A good father will help lead and guide his children in the purpose that God has for their life. This is the very essence of being a father. The absence of knowing your purpose produces loneliness, frustration, disappointments, a sense of failure and many negative results. People can go to school for many years, to work for additional years in professions that can end in great disappointment simply because they never discovered their purpose. Cemeteries are filled with people who died with regrets never knowing why they lived. It is the discovery of your purpose that produces great satisfaction and turns a dangerous crisis into a challenging opportunity for God to show up.

I left my fathers presence that day feeling utterly dejected, but determined to prove him wrong about me. With an air of urgency and importance, I told my friends as we gazed across the Accra airport runway, "I am simply fed up with Ghana; I am tired of this land." It was of no consequence to me whether they believed me or not. Every young man I knew had made plans to go to America or Europe in search of a better life. As far as I knew, that was the only route to success and recognition, and I was not going to be left out of the race.

Like most young people, at the time I didn't understand my father's opinion of me and I wanted to impress him by proving he was wrong regardless of what counsel he gave me to lead me back to a proven path of academic success. I wanted to show him that I could get ahead in life without his instructions.

I was about to find out that life has a way of teaching you the lessons you refuse to learn from parental wisdom.

CHAPTER 05

STOWAWAY LESSONS

"A man's heart deviseth his way: but the Lord directeth his steps." (Proverbs 16:9)

Stowaway to France

Soon after the conversation with my father my plans for going to Europe were complete. There was no going back. Because of the dangerous nature of my plan of action I thought it wise to conceal my scheme from my parents and close associates.

Two routes were open to me. The first possibility was to travel by air, but I readily ruled out that option because I did not have a visa or enough money to buy an airplane ticket. The second option was to stow away on a foreign ship bound for Europe. This was extremely dangerous. There were many stories about Ghanaian boys who stowed away on foreign ships only to be cast overboard by the ship's captain to be mauled and killed by sharks. For nights, I lay sleepless calculating the risk involved in what I was about to do. "This could mean life or death," I thought to myself, "but there is no way out for me." My mind was made up!

To avoid detection by my parents and friends, I wrapped a couple of shirts and trousers in a polythene bag and headed for the lorry station before daybreak.

"Which vehicle is going to Kumasi?" I enquired with a shivering voice. The officials pointed to a government transport (public transportation) en route to Kumasi. I quickly boarded it for the first leg of my trip to greener pastures. The second leg was from Kumasi to Abidjan, the capital of Côte d'Ivoire, where I was presented with a problem: I did not speak French. This did not deter me, however, because I viewed myself as a passenger in transit. Once I arrived, I found a place to stay in Abidjan. I made some Ghanaian friends who were also planning to stowaway and we studied how it was done together. Eventually I managed to smuggle on board a ship headed for France. I squeezed myself amongst a pile of timber logs stowed on deck. I had hidden some French bread in some long goalkeeper's socks and had also carefully stowed a small container of water. It was enough, I hoped, to last an uncertain number of days. To beat security, I donned all my clothing - two pairs of trousers, two heavy-duty shirts, two sweaters and two coats. I thought I was set for life in the logs.

Then, as often is the case, the unexpected happened. I had been lying down in between the logs of wood for several days and nights. Although, as far as I could tell, there was really no difference between the day and night. I was under complete self-imposed restriction laying in the same position the entire time. Then suddenly unexpected torrential rains came down and my fortitude and courage were stretched to the limit. I was suddenly faced with the grim reality of dying from exposure and hunger in the midst of the logs. As the ship tossed turbulently, seawater washed over the logs where I was hiding. The only option open to me was to come out and surrender to the ship's captain, which might mean death. As I stretched and stepped out of hiding, I came face to face with other stowaways amidst the logs who had also been forced to surrender by the unexpected storm.

Needless to say, the captain of the ship was already commanding the captured stowaways to jump ship one by one and swim to shore in the treacherous shark infested waters. He seemed set to cast us all overboard when the chief mate of the ship appeared on the scene and started asking our names.

"My name is Nicholas," I said humbly as he approached me. Suddenly the chief mate stopped in his tracks. He gazed into my eyes. My thoughts were racing wildly. I felt like I was standing on a precipice ready to be pushed to my death. After a pause, he said, "My son is also called Nicholas."

> *"If I take the wings of the dawn, If I dwell in the remotest part of the sea, Even there Your hand will lead me, And Your right hand will lay hold of me." (Psalm 139:9-10)*

It was like a miracle! He stopped asking the rest of the stowaways for their names and walked over to the captain. After a lengthy argument and some angry gesticulations from the captain, the possibility of the death sentence was squashed. We were marched without further interrogation to a cargo hold beneath the ship. Despite the fact that it was like a dungeon without adequate light and food, it was unquestionably better than lying among the logs.

This was just one of the early signs of God's providence in my life. God saw that I was attempting to enforce my prophetic destiny. Now that I have been to Europe many times and stayed in some of the finest places, I realize that I was fighting for the future that was already secured for me by God! But, God in His wisdom would not permit it to be obtained in the flesh. Beloved, the future you see for yourself is a sure promise from God. But, don't be fooled by the enticing allure of worldly gain. The method does not justify the means.

> *"For what is a man profited, if he shall gain the whole world, and lose his own soul? or what shall a man give in exchange for his soul?" (Matthew 16:26)*

Sent Back Home

Finally, when the ship reached France and berthed at the port of Marseilles, we were released with a stern warning not to disclose our identity in town. We found harbor jobs to keep body and soul together. But I was in search of deeper adventures, and that meant I needed to make more money. Before I could do anything about it, however, the police arrested me as they swooped down on a company of rioting port workers. This time, the officials were bent on deporting me back to Ghana. On my homebound journey, I was put on another ship to Barcelona in Spain and then to Dakar in Senegal. The French officials there put me aboard a plane, a Pan Am flight, which was destined for Accra.

As soon as the aircraft touched the runway in Accra, I made up my mind to pull a fast one on my father. I could not bear to disclose to him the details of my abortive stowaway attempt and consequent deportation -- I was still very much ruled by the strong vow I had made to prove to him that I could be successful without his endorsement. Therefore, with the little amount of foreign currency I had on me I bought a giant-sized bottle of Johnnie Walker and presented it to my father under the pretext that I had just flown in from John F. Kennedy International Airport in New York. I lied to save face and to impress him. I don't think my father believed me. In fact, he said to my other siblings, "Your brother says he has just arrived from America. Here we go again." I had failed yet again to please him.

Stowaway To Israel

The days and weeks after my deportation were difficult. I was gripped with uneasiness and frustration, and I itched to go back to Europe. As soon as possible and before my money was completely gone, I traveled by road to Abidjan where once again I smuggled myself aboard a ship. After a few days on the high seas, I surrendered to the captain with the hope that he would consider me for a job. Instead, I was locked up.

Cargo was removed as we made a port stop in Haifa, Israel. When we got to Haifa, Israel I broke out of the prison in the ship's hold and I sneaked into town. The security was too tight and I could not speak or understand the language and I didn't see anyone like me or anyone I could talk to. But, even with my limited knowledge, I knew that the land of Israel held great significance. Which is why as I looked out over my surroundings, I remember thinking about who God is and whether He knew about my life. I challenged God to deliver me, to prove himself in my life if He is truly the God that the Bible says He is. In hindsight, I did not know then how powerful this thought was, and at this point I did not know the power of prayer. After that year, I got saved and would go on to a life of prayer.

I was only disembarked for a short while and when I did not find a face like mine in the crowd, I went back and turned myself in to the ship's captain and was locked up right away and brought back to Ghana, arriving at the port city, Takoradi.

The rest of that year was devoted to working out new schemes to achieve the lofty goals that were sprouting in my mind. Meanwhile, my company of friends multiplied and I spared no efforts in telling them glowing stories of the charm and beauty of Europe based on my faint recollections and great visions and dreams of a life beyond Ghana. I didn't realize at the time that I was prophesying the great future God had in store for me.

> *"For I know the plans I have for you,"*
> *declares the LORD, "plans to prosper you*
> *and not to harm you, plans to give you*
> *hope and a future." (Jeremiah 29:11)*

CHAPTER 06

ALTARS OF SACRIFICE

There are many devices in a man's heart; nevertheless the counsel of the Lord, that shall stand. (Proverbs 19:21)

The Executioner

One night I was attending a gathering at a house of my father's that was being used by my uncle as a hotel in Kumasi. A very intimidating looking man had gotten drunk and was disturbing the other guests. My aunty asked me to get the man a taxi and get him off the premises. My aunty followed us to the road to hail the taxi. When the car came, my aunty jumped in the back with the man and I innocently jumped in the front seat with the driver to take the man to his destination safely.

Unbeknownst to me, my aunty and the man who was known in our local dialect as an "ɔbrafo", which in the English is best translated as an "Executioner" for the Shrine or the place where sacrifices are made.

There are times and seasons when people die in some religions that a human sacrifice is requested by the shrine and such people called an "ɔbrafo" or "executioner" are deployed to collect human heads to be buried with the deceased body. The belief is that someone must be taken to "serve the dead person" as they journey through the underworld. So the person to be sacrificed is beheaded by the "ɔbrafo" or executioner and their body is preserved through embalming and kept in the shrine. I did not know any of this at that time.

As we rode along the highway and traveled some kilometers from my father's hotel, I heard my aunty and the executioner discussing something feverishly in the local dialect in the backseat but I was not paying attention.

Apparently my aunty and the executioner were debating in a heated argument. My aunty was saying that since "Kojo Duncan" (my father) was a royal it was not possible to use his son for the sacrifice that the executioner was making. The executioner was saying a head is a head and blood is blood and that it is necessary that they present a head at this time. In fact, he insisted that since the young man (me) was the son of a royal, this made me even more valuable. Per the tradition, the royals and their descendants are considered a more valuable prize as a sacrifice.

Suddenly, as we went to turn at the junction right before reaching the shrine doors......POW!!!! The tire blew on the taxi and I jumped out with the driver to help change the spare tire.

When I got out the taxi driver said, "Listen, what is wrong with you? You are the one they are talking about! They are going to go sacrifice you! If you enter that place you are not coming back!"

I said, "Please, forget it. This is my aunty."

He said, "Don't be fooled. I am from the stool house. I know what they do here. If you enter, you are not coming back alive. Run!"

I leaned into the taxi and told my aunty I needed to use the restroom. I then took off and ran as fast as I could and caught a taxi at the next junction back to my father who was still at the hotel in Kumasi.

When I arrived there, he said "Nick, where have you been?" I told him what had happened. He looked at me intently and said.... "You. You are a miracle. You are born to live." He then told me the explanation of what the assignment of the "executioner" is to present heads during times of burial. I was indeed rescued.

Divine Escapes

Once again the providence of God rescued me by way of untimely circumstances – this time a blown tire. My friend, Jesus said "And a man's foes shall be they of his own household." (Matthew 10:36) At this time, I didn't even know anything about altars or covenants. I did not know the truth written in scripture that declares: "Blessed be the Lord, who hath not given us as a prey to their teeth. Our soul is escaped as a bird out of the snare of the fowlers: the snare is broken, and we are escaped." (Psalm 124:6-7)

It is situations like these in the natural that have given me understanding to pray and have revelation in the spirit. Many times when I am praying for someone, the Spirit will reveal that they are dealing with a family altar or a covenant that is calling for sacrifice. The sacrifice may be their marriage, their children, their finances or even their life that is being requested by the altar. But, do not be afraid of such requests because the Bible shows us in Judges 6 how to deal with family altars.

In Judges 6 Gideon deals with his father's altar and it sets the course first for his father's freedom, then his family's freedom, and then ultimately the freedom of the whole nation. In Judges 6:26 God instructs Gideon to tear down the altar of his father and present a new sacrifice and raise an altar to God. When the men of the city awake to see what has happened and discover it was Gideon who did it, they appeal to the father to present his son as a sacrifice. His father could've gone on worshipping Baal (the god of the family altar) and sacrificed Gideon, but he takes a different decision and the men, along with Gideon's family, get involved in a strategic battle that unseats the seven-year oppression of the Midianites and sets the entire nation of Israel free.

Do not be afraid to contend for your family and tear down altars of destruction by raising a new altar to God through sacrificing and fervent prayer. At this time, I was not aware that years later I would draw on these rich experiences to understand spiritual warfare and the battle strategies of the enemy.

It is during this time that ideas about God and the meaning of creation began to flood my mind with great urgency. The more I fought these thoughts; the more fear and anxiety assailed me. Suddenly, it struck me that there must be something supernatural about my life and all the events that unfolded from my birth until now. I set my heart to understand why these things were happening in my life. The quest to understand opened me up further to be introduced to characters that were willing to take me to extremes to find the answer. The enemy was more than willing to assist me in this endeavor by assigning his own agents. Once again I made new friends. These friends introduced me to marijuana, nicotine and alcohol. These vices helped to temporarily soothe some of my fears and anxieties. However, deep down in me, the insatiable quest to search for a solution only deepened.

Soon after this, I took a trip with one of my new friends to the Western Region of Ghana, where we walked for several kilometers through thick tropical forest to a popular shrine. The fetish priest welcomed me with glee. He set at work to consult his gods about my fate. Suddenly, the priest shot out of his inner court to the reception area and stared at me. He went into the inner court again, this time performing frenzied dancing and gaggling of a weird nature. When he came out again, he had a cold lifeless look in his eyes.

"Young man, who are you?" he asked.

I stammered a reply, "Eh, I am from Accra."

He did not seem satisfied with my answer. "I say, tell me who you are now!" He was very agitated.

Cold fear ran through my body, but I managed to say, "Please I am a young man from Accra who wants your gods to help me succeed in life."

The fetish priest shook his baldhead several times and then tossed his staff. He said to me, "Young man, I cannot do anything for you." He pointed to the sky and said, "The only one who can help you is the man upstairs." Meaning the God of Heaven. After that he asked me to leave.

His words filled me with fear, confusion and anxiety. By his expression and his vehement declaration, I was more determined to search for an answer and find the "God Factor". I did not know then as I know now, that God's providence was protecting me from destruction. I went to an ambassador of Satan --- the very thing that was seeking my destruction. But God protected me!

Looking For God

Further visits to various "spiritualist" only brought more confusion as I was introduced to the spirit world. At one point I went to a shrine that asked me to bring a close loved one for a blood sacrifice. I told the fetish priest I could not do such a thing and I refused to bring the sacrifice. As I left with my friend, he said "Nick, no one tells (that particular fetish priest) they will not bring a requested sacrifice and survives." I said I could not and would not do it and I left. I decided to go to church and seek the help I was not getting from these so-called spiritual guides.

At that time, there were no Charismatic Churches and no one who could teach me about deliverance. Many mainstream churches I attended did not or could not help. They only stirred up more questions about life rather than provided any answers. Though not yet saved, I began to have a strong sense that God had a plan for my life.

I did not know, nor had I ever read, the following Scripture:

> *For ye see your calling, brethren, how that not many wise men after the flesh, not many mighty, not many noble, are called: But God hath chosen the foolish things of the world to confound the wise; and God hath chosen the weak things of the world to confound the things which are mighty; And base things of the world, and things which are despised, had God chosen yea, and things which are not, to bring to naught things that are: That no flesh should glory in his presence. (1 Cor. 1:26-29)*

In my ignorance and frustration at the lack of a real solution, I shunned any idea of God despite the strong sense I had of Him calling me. I prepared a discotheque attendance schedule, which I posted atop of my bed, and dutifully committed myself to having all the fun and fame life could offer. Along with my friends, I went from cinemas to discos night after night. We graduated from lower degrees of sin to higher levels of iniquity. I had made a plan to live my life my own way.

As I think back over this period of my life, with so many timely divine escapes, it amazes and humbles me to see what God has done with my life. He has been faithful.

"It is of the Lord's mercies that we are not consumed, because his compassions fail not. They are new every morning: great is thy faithfulness." Lamentations 3:22-23

CHAPTER 07

PAIN REVEALS A NEW BEGINNING

"For when we were yet without strength, in due time Christ died for the ungodly... But God commendeth his love toward us, in that, while we were yet sinners, Christ died for us. (Romans 5:6,8)

The Traditions of Men

Tradition is very powerful. Every community the world over has a deep respect for its cultural and religious practices. While it may seem very strange in other cultures, traditional religious practices are still practiced in many nations and not all nations practice Christianity. This was definitely the norm in Ghana as I was growing up. There were as many shrines as there were various types of churches. People have different cultural and religious practices the world over. I know now what I did not know then. When you are born in such cultures, you may be practicing some of the traditions you have been introduced to, but you must be willing to break away from your traditions in order to enforce the Word of God.

> *"God, who at sundry times and in divers manners spake in time past unto the fathers by the prophets, Hath in these last days spoken unto us by his Son, whom he hath appointed heir of all things, by whom also he made the worlds..." (Hebrews 1:1-2)*

The Apostle Paul spoke about his own cultural and religious practices before coming to Christ in Galatians 1:13-15 – *"For ye have heard of my conversation in time past in the Jews' religion, how that beyond measure I persecuted the church of God, and wasted it: And profited in the Jews' religion above many my equals in mine own nation, being more exceedingly zealous of the traditions of my fathers. But when it pleased God, who separated me from my mother's womb, and called me by his grace..."*

No matter how cherished your traditional values are to you, NEVER resist the voice of God because of them. There are a lot of people in church today who because of some practices handed down to them from their forebears refuse to marry from certain ethnic groups; consider some foods as taboo, and practice other things such as palm reading or following daily horoscopes. We are from different families and ethnic backgrounds with specific upbringing of varying traditions and customs. But let the WORD of God be supreme whenever you are seeking a deeper understanding of God Himself.

> *"For laying aside the commandment of God, ye hold the tradition of men, as the washing of pots and cups: and many other such like things ye do. And he said unto them, Full well ye reject the commandment of God, that ye may keep your own tradition." (Mark 7:8-9)*

In my search for God and the subsequent visits to the shrines, to various spiritual churches, in addition to trying to appease the fears, anxieties and mental torment through self-medicating with marijuana and alcohol --- I worsened my state of mind and opened up my spirit to be accessed by the powers of darkness.

Some of the evil spirits I had consulted in various places began to torment and haunt me every night. I could not sleep. I heard all kinds of weird voices tempting me to commit suicide. I eventually lost control of myself. I knew I needed help but did not know how or where to find it. I was on a mission to find the meaning and purpose of my life. In my search, the year of my salvation will forever remain etched in my mind.

My Hand in the Fire

It was truly the year of new beginnings in my life. One night, I could hardly sleep because of the demonic attacks. I was under great stress and I was suffering hallucinations. A voice commanded me to light a candle in my bedroom, so I did. The voice once again commanded me to stick my right palm upon the blazing flame of the candle. For some reason, I momentarily lost all consciousness of pain as my fingers roasted upon the candle flame. My senses were lulled. Any reflex I might have had to withdraw my hand was lost as I yielded completely to the evil voices.

Then, suddenly, I came to myself and was deluged with agonizing pain. It was unbearable. I could not believe my eyes - my three right middle fingers were burnt like mashed meat. Blood oozed out profusely from the stumps of my fingers. It was as if something or someone had taken my ability to speak and I could not call for help or remove my hand from the fire. I heard a voice saying I could not take my fingers off the fire until the candle was completely burned out.

But suddenly, against the command saying for me to hold my hand in the fire until the candle burned out, the excruciating pain pushed me to breakthrough with a shout!

"Help me! Help me! I am dying!"

Through my excruciating pain, I heard the sound of footsteps approaching my door and heard someone forcefully flinging it open. At that point I passed out. When I awoke, I found myself firmly strapped to a bed in Ward 8 of the Korle Bu Teaching Hospital in Accra. A nurse standing by my bed held my uninjured hand and said to me, "Nick, you narrowly escaped death."

Because I had a history of abuse of marijuana and other substances my injury was attributed to such things in my medical records. It was later I realized that my injuries were truly the result of extreme spiritual torment. With revelation today I can understand that a messenger of Satan had been assigned to buffet my flesh and torment me from my birth up until now in order to abort my divine destiny if it had been possible. But the assignment was overruled.

> *"And lest I should be exalted above measure through the abundance of the revelations, there was given to me a thorn in the flesh, the messenger of Satan to buffet me, lest I should be exalted above measure." (2 Cor. 12:7)*

CHAPTER 08

SALVATION

"Come to Me, all you who labor and are heavy laden, and I will give you rest." (Matthew 11:28)

The Bed of Affliction

Four months in the bed of affliction offered me plenty of opportunity to reflect on my whole life. My so-called friends, both male and female, were all gone. No one came to visit me or consoled me from my previous life of adventure. My father was the only one who came to see me. I felt alone, confused and abandoned.

The disco and nightclub life meant nothing to me with my heavily bandaged hand. All the questions that lay dormant in my mind resurfaced. In fact my mind was sober and all the temporary distractions gave way to a flood of the thoughts of my new reality. What is life all about? Where does a man go to after death? Is this all there is to life? Are we all pawns at the mercy of blind fate and forces beyond our control? My soul was not at rest. I was searching for something. But thank God! Jesus said, *"Come to Me, all you who labor and are heavy laden, and I will give you rest."* (Matthew 11:28).

My life was about to change forever. Job 14:14-15 says, *"If a man die, shall he live again? all the days of my appointed time will I wait, till my change come. Thou shalt call, and I will answer thee: thou wilt have a desire to the work of thine hands."* The old man had passed away in my affliction and the new man was about to come on the scene.

Salvation Comes

One day, an Indian woman by the name of Mrs. Rajj came to preach the gospel of Jesus Christ to me. With her were the Acquah sisters and some Christian nurses at Korle Bu Teaching Hospital, who boldly shared the Good News of God's saving grace and deliverance with me.

As the days passed, a newfound peace flooded my soul. To my amazement, my restlessness abated. The Acquah sisters labored patiently to explain the difficult questions I raised. When I was discharged that December, I knew beyond any shadow of a doubt that I had become a new man in Christ Jesus. I spent hours searching the Word of God to understand the mysteries of His knowledge.

As soon as I got saved and was discharged I became very zealous for God. One of the Acquah sisters took me to the Church of Pentecost where I started attending "Dawn broadcasting", all night prayer services, outreach ministry, and winning souls and bringing people to church.

I devoted whole days to fasting and praying to know the will of God for my life. Now that I had finally accepted His Son, God was working rapidly on my behalf. I intended in my heart to be steadfast and faithful in my commitment to God and His church. I walked several kilometers every day to attend the Church of Pentecost fellowship meetings. The kilometers felt like mere yards as I sang and prayed in tongues all the way to and from church.

I was winning souls and inviting others to church and it felt good. I started evangelism and outreach by visiting the universities and secondary schools reaching out to the students, preaching Christ and giving them my testimony. I was really on fire for God. It started spreading all over town that I had become an evangelist and was winning souls for Jesus.

> *"And as ye go, preach, saying, The kingdom of heaven is at hand. Heal the sick, cleanse the lepers, raise the dead, cast out devils: freely ye have received, freely give..." (Matthew 10:7-8)*

CHAPTER 09

A NEW LIFE IN CHRIST

"Study to shew thyself approved unto God, a workman that needeth not to be ashamed, rightly dividing the word of truth." (2 Timothy 2:15)

Bible School in Benin City

Zeal for the Lord absorbed my life. Day and night, my mind was filled with evangelism and the things of God. As I sat one evening watching a "Redemption Hour" television program in Accra, the famous Nigerian international evangelist, Rev. Dr. Benson Idahosa preached a sermon inspired by the Holy Ghost, which he concluded with an invitation to Ghanaians who wished to be trained in the Charismatic-oriented Bible School to come to Nigeria and apply for the training program. The Lord said immediately to my heart, "Apply and go, for I have opened a door for you."

I did, and so began my formal training and progress in ministry. With a full scholarship from Rev. Dr. Idahosa, I spent my days knowing that I was in the perfect will of God. The Bible School in Benin City, Nigeria, offered me a great opportunity to test my academic faculties, but, because of my lack of formal education, I had serious challenges coping with the rigorous academic work. What really sustained me was my dependence upon God in prayer and, of course, the personal encouragement accorded me by the Rev. Dr. Idahosa (who later became Archbishop Idahosa) and who had by then become my mentor.

He saw greatness in me that I did not see at that time. Great spiritual fathers can see promise in sons and daughters. It is through submission to your spiritual father that ministry gifts can be pulled out and developed.

Paul said in 1st Corinthians 4:14-15, *"I write not these things to shame you, but as my beloved sons I warn you. For though ye have ten thousand instructors in Christ, yet have ye not many fathers: for in Christ Jesus I have begotten you through the gospel."* God will favor us with a spiritual father to help us as we grow and develop in ministry.

Favor is a powerful weapon against the lack of having had my father's guidance from birth. Archbishop Idahosa took a special interest in me and became my spiritual father to help raise me in the things of the Spirit and teach me lessons I had not learned during my youth. Having a spiritual father is critical to the discovery and fulfillment of one's divine purpose in life.

My friend, happy is the man who finds his purpose in life. Loneliness is not the absence of people. Loneliness is the absence of purpose. Once you find your purpose, you will find what will bring your life divine fulfillment. Despite all my earlier experiences and challenges, I had finally found my purpose!

Church of Pentecost

Upon my return to Ghana, I went back to the Church of Pentecost, where I had started fellowship after my conversion. I sought to be engaged as an evangelist with the church but the church was not ready at that time for me to work as an evangelist for the church. The head of the church, Rev. James McKeown, explained to me the negative experiences the church had gone through with evangelists and similar situations.

For some time, I felt discouraged and dejected. But one thing the Church of Pentecost and the Bible School developed in me was the zeal for prayer. Studying under Archbishop Idahosa meant that you did not give up on things easily. I decided to go back to the schools where I had been before going to school in Nigeria and to keep reaching out. My relationship and continual communication with my spiritual father, Rev. Dr. Idahosa helped me to develop inner tenacity and to draw upon the resilience I had learned as an adolescent. I remained determined to work for God in spite of the apparent setback, so I consulted with a few senior ministers. They all supported me as I pursued what God had laid on my heart to do.

Ministry Beginnings

Once I started the ministry, the battle was not over. Indeed, the battle had just truly started. Remember I told you that the many prophecies you receive are an opening for the enemy to wage war. But, every battle we are willing to fight, God will open the door for new opportunities.

It does not matter how far we think we've come, there are vast opportunities that God has for us. God does not want us to settle for the place we are today. He wants us to rise up and take possession of the promises He has made to us.

Before Moses died in the plains of Moab, the Lord took him *"...to the top of Pisgah, which is across from Jericho. And the LORD showed him all the land of Gilead as far as Dan, all Naphtali and the land of Ephraim and Manasseh, all the land of Judah as far as the Western Sea, the South, and the plain of the Valley of Jericho, the city of palm trees, as far as Zoar. Then the LORD said to him, "This is the land of which I swore to give Abraham, Isaac, and Jacob, saying, 'I will give it to your descendants."* (Deuteronomy 34:1-4)

When Joshua assumed the leadership, the promise was still in force and all he needed to do, was to prepare; move from where he was; cross over the Jordan and possess the land. Though they had broken the chains of intimidation and frustration and had lifted the burdens of Egypt from off their shoulders, that was not enough. They had to rise up and array themselves in the garments of warfare and engage the armies of the enemies of Zion in battle; dispossess them and possess their lands. As far as God was concerned, the inhabitants of the nations and cities beyond the Jordan were illegal occupants and they had to be subdued. The possession of the lands had already been declared as shown in the Scripture above. But they had to contend for them.

Many people have asked why we go through so much spiritual warfare. When your future has been declared and that future is great – the enemy will also make declarations to cause the plan of God to be aborted or delayed. But, you must be willing to fight for what God has promised. We do not battle against flesh and blood, but we do battle. We must fight the good fight of faith and contend for our divine promises.

> *Ephesians 6:12 says, "For we wrestle not against flesh and blood, but against principalities, against powers, against the rulers of the darkness of this world, against spiritual wickedness in high places."*

Beloved, God will not deny you of the blessings He's promised you; He will not withhold the miracles He's assured you of. The blessings have already been given and the benedictions have been conferred on you. All that is left is for you to rise up; engage the enemies who are hindering their manifestations. I challenge you to pray more than ever before and take action concerning the promises of God and you will be a living example to your generation to the glory of God.

CHAPTER 10

THE BIRTH OF CHRISTIAN ACTION FAITH MINISTRIES

"Being confident of this very thing, that he which hath begun a good work in you will perform it until the day of Jesus Christ." (Philippians 1:6)

The Various Locations

I began to organize Saturday prayer meetings in my father's house at the Airport Residential area. Along the way, Archbishop Idahosa sent Rev. J. S. B. Coker to assist me in the work I had begun doing. As the months passed my ministry grew and I started Sunday services at the Association School in Accra.

The church, which I later named Christian Action Faith Ministries, began to grow. We moved from the Association School, from there to "Student's Hostel", the diplomatic shop at the airport residential area and then to Teachers Hall then on to Trade Fair.

From there, we experienced steady growth, so we moved from the Trade Fair site, and finally to our present location at the Spintex Road in Accra.

As a result of the visible miracles, healings and great teachings on Faith and Prosperity, many young people came from the schools and colleges, as well as adults from the mainstream churches. Today, many of these young people have also pioneered churches, with some already ordained as Bishops and General Overseers. By God's grace, the influence of the ministry has gone far, both nationally and internationally.

Historic Recognition

One chronicler of Church History in Ghana, Susan Hanson, sums it all up in her book, **A Nation Touched By The Fire of Heaven:** "Today, the Christian Action Faith Ministries has churches in almost every continent of the world. [Rev. Duncan-Williams] is also the Presiding Bishop and General Overseer. The 'mega' church at it headquarters, attracts crowds in the thousands in a typical Sunday service. Many lives have been transformed, given purpose and direction, and God has used Rev. Duncan-Williams in several miracles, healings and signs. He has seen the power of God move in diverse ways. He also wields much influence in governmental circles.

Affectionately called 'The People's Bishop,' one can confidently say that Bishop Duncan-Williams is one Charismatic minister who literally 'junkets' the whole world with the gospel message, holding several meetings outside the shores of this country."

CHAPTER 11

WHAT TO DO IN TIMES OF CRISIS

"For I reckon that the sufferings of this present time are not worthy to be compared with the glory which shall be revealed in us." (Romans 8:18)

Crisis Can Happen in Ministry

As much as I have had successes in ministry, I have also had some challenging times in ministry as well as in my personal life. I have been the center of attention and some of my challenges have covered national newspapers. Even friends and loved ones have withdrawn from me and on occasion betrayed me. During some of my greatest challenges, even some of my sons and daughters in whom I have nursed in the spirit of love and care in the ministry refused to reciprocate the love and refrained from caring for my hurting soul. I have sometimes felt very lonely in ministry.

It is times like these; I will spend a lot of time staying vigil through the watches of the night praying for the Spirit of Elohim to direct me to make good decisions. I have learned not to take any decision based on my feelings and the emotional waves surging at the time of these difficulties. Until I hear from Elohim, I won't take a step regardless of the pressure.

My advice, from experience, is that when challenges come your way, this is not the time to make decisions without first spending time tarrying before the Lord and waiting for a fresh infilling from the Spirit of God. Jesus was filled with the Spirit and led by the Spirit BEFORE He entered a 40-day Fast.

> *"And Jesus being full of the Holy Ghost returned from Jordan, and was led by the Spirit into the wilderness." (Luke 4:1)*

He didn't confront the wilderness or deal with the strategies of the enemy until He had Spiritual Clearance.

Offenses and Mastering Betrayal

It is the rejection, pain and judgment of others during times of crisis that open you up and expose you to the spirit of offense. Offense is defined as a "stumbling-block". It will cause you to err and can even make your situation worse.

Jesus said that offenses are inevitable:

> *"Then said he unto the disciples, It is impossible but that offences will come: but woe unto him, through whom they come!" (Luke 17:1)*

As this scripture says, offenses will come, but we must work not to let them come through us. We can experience things in life that will make us even wonder if God sees and knows how we are being mistreated. When John the Baptist was about to be beheaded, he sent his disciples to question the authenticity of Jesus and scripture says, *"Jesus said blessed is whosoever is not offended in me: "And blessed is he, whosoever shall not be offended in me." (Matthew 11:6).*

This scripture shows us there is a blessing in walking without offense. We must master offenses if we are going to have a successful walk in our Christian life. Indeed Proverbs 19:11 says, *"Good sense makes one slow to anger, and it is his glory to overlook an offense."* So whenever you get offended, you stand to lose a blessing and it is to your glory to overlook a transgression.

Final Advice When Crisis Comes

During one major crisis in my life and ministry, I went to see my spiritual grandfather in the Lord, the great Evangelist Dr. T. L. Osborne and he gave me advice I still follow to this day:

"Don't defend yourself. You are not on trial. If you defend yourself, you will give people the power to judge you. Never try to explain yourself. Remember it takes two or more people to agree. Don't agree with the predictions of your critics. Just stay in the throne room my son. You will recover if you will stay in the throne room. Stay in the throne room my son. Remain anointed and the oil will answer your critics. Pursue your calling with passion as if nothing has happened."

When challenges come your way --- Don't leave the throne room. Stay passionate about your calling. Feed your faith and starve your doubts. Remember, even when situations don't favor you or people don't choose you - you are still chosen by God. Don't agree with those who criticize, condemn and complain about who God made you.

Keep advancing and pursuing the call and purpose of God for your life. You are blessed!

CHAPTER 12

PRAY WITH ME

Prayer Points

I decree and declare the release of my promise and that I possess the faith and tenacity to wage war against the enemy at the gate, the adversaries at the door and anyone holding my keys to victory in the name of Jesus.

I decree and declare the establishment of His Kingdom and decree the Will of God over my life, my family, my church and my nation in the name of Jesus.

I decree and declare I will not be a victim of circumstances and I won't rest until I have obtained the promises of God for my family, community, church and nation in the name of Jesus.

I release by Divine Authority my divine helpers to wage war on the enemy and silence the voice of those around me who operate in sowing fear, disbelief and doubt to keep me from my divine inheritance in the name of Jesus.

I interrupt and destroy devices that are designed to operate, oppose and hinder my ability, movements, divine strategies that will enable me to obtain total and complete victory in the name of Jesus.

By the Supreme Sacrifice of the Blood of Jesus, I take possession of the gates of the enemy and secure the gates of The Righteous in the name of Jesus.

I arrest every projection, inhibition; embargo and restriction of the wicked designed to manipulate, destroy, delay, deny or subvert the release of my total victory and appointed promises in the name of Jesus.

Prayer of Salvation

God, I recognize that I have not lived my life for You up until now. I have been living for myself and that is wrong. I have read the scripture in Romans 10:9-10 which says, "That if thou shalt confess with thy mouth the Lord Jesus, and shalt believe in thine heart that God hath raised him from the dead, thou shalt be saved. For with the heart man believeth unto righteousness; and with the mouth confession is made unto salvation." Today I deploy the scripture and confess I want You to save me. I am a sinner in need of a Savior. Erase my name from the Book of Death and write my name in the Lamb's Book of Life. Seal me unto the Day of Redemption. I need You in my life; I want You in my life. I acknowledge the completed work of Your Son Jesus Christ in giving His life for me on the cross at Calvary, and I long to receive the forgiveness you have made freely available to me through this sacrifice. Come into my life now, Lord. Take up residence in my heart and be my king, my Lord, and my Savior. From this day forward, I will no longer be controlled by sin, or the desire to please myself, but I will follow You all the days of my life. Save me Lord. Help me find a good church and locate a good Spiritual family of God that will help me grow in the knowledge of God and fulfill my divine call. Thank you Lord! In Jesus Name. Amen.

www.ingramcontent.com/pod-product-compliance
Lightning Source LLC
Chambersburg PA
CBHW070518090426
42735CB00012B/2829